Table of Contents

Title Page..1
About the Publisher..3
Introduction 5
Poem 1 - The Death of a Rose..7
Poem 2 - Just Being. 11
Poem 3 - What Ends. 13
Poem 4 - The Monk's Dichotomy. 15
Poem 5 - The Monk and the Villagers. 17
Poem 6 - The Unseen Gift. 21
Poem 7 - Twenty-two Flowers. 23
Poem 8 - The Green Rose. 25
Poem 09 - Odin's Heir. 27
Poem 10 - Secrets of the Dark Side. 29
Poem 11 - Meditation Under Desire. 31
Poem 12 - The Purpose of Insanity. 33
Poem 13 - Beyond Betrayal. 35
Poem 14 - When Beauty Fades Away. 37
Poem 15 - The Way of the Rose. 39
Poem 16 - The Surprise of Losing You. 41
Poem 17 - Knowing Without Power. 43
Poem 18 - I Apologize!. 45
Poem 19 - If You Could Contemplate. 47
Poem 20 - Curse. 49
Poem 21 - A Prisoner of Insanity. 51
Poem 22 - Entanglement. 53
Poem 23 - Ascension. 55
Poem 24 - World of Sinners. 57
Poem 25 - Being Someone I'm Not. 59
Poem 26 - The Desire You Chose. 61
Poem 27 - How to Love Someone. 63
Poem 28 - Lovely. 65
Poem 29 - The Way of the Lost. 67
Poem 30 - The Seductive Demon. 69

Poem 31 - The Fear of The Feared. ... 71
Poem 32 - Wandering. ... 73
Poem 33 - The Mask. ... 75
Poem 34 - Unfinished World. ... 77
Poem 35 - Desire. ... 79
Poem 36 - The Meaning of Life. ... 81
Poem 37 - The Colors of Love. ... 83
Poem 38 - I Wish. ... 85
Poem 39 - So Far and So Near. ... 87
Poem 40 - If You Loved Me. ... 89
Poem 41 - I Don't Believe You. ... 91
Poem 42 - Your Sword. ... 93
Poem 43 - Bewitched. ... 95
Poem 44 - Queen of the Dark. ... 97
Poem 45 - Affliction. ... 99
Poem 46 - Who Can Free Me? ... 101
Poem 47 - Slayer. ... 103
Poem 48 - Complicity. ... 105
Poem 49 - Empty Promises. ... 107
Poem 50 - The Victory of the Vanquished. ... 109
Poem 51 - Adrift. ... 111
Poem 52 - Where I Found Myself. ... 113
Poem 53 - The Muse. ... 115
Poem 54 - Unable to Be. ... 117
Poem 55 - The Cross of Light. ... 119
Poem 56 - Reverberations. ... 121
Poem 57 - Hidden World. ... 123
Poem 58 - The Love I Fear. ... 125
Poem 59 - Treacherous. ... 127
Poem 60 - The Fate of the Damned. ... 129
Poem 61 - I Hate this Existence. ... 131
Poem 62 - Because I Cannot Love. ... 133
Poem 63 - I Believe You are Good. ... 135
Poem 64 - Please Be Free! ... 137
Poem 65 - Shoot an Arrow! ... 139

Poem 66 - Nowadays.	141
Poem 67 - Our Empire.	143
Poem 68 - Come and See!.	145
Poem 69 - Omnia In Divina.	147
Poem 70 - Life Has Pain.	149
Poem 71 - What a Lie Can't Conquer.	151
Poem 72 - Magic.	153
Poem 73 - No Future Holds the Mind.	155
Poem 74 - Saints and Sinners.	157
Poem 75 - Incomprehensible.	159
Poema 76 - The Nothing You Represent.	161
Poem 77 - Why Love?	163
Poem 78 - A Thousand Sensations.	165
Poem 79 - An Intrigue.	167
Poem 80 - Pride.	169
Poem 81 - Lucifer.	171
Poem 82 - Stupidity.	173
Poem 83 - Seeing Myself in You.	175
Poem 84 - Dispensable.	177
Poem 85 - The Damnable.	179
Poem 86 - Illusory Love.	181
Poem 87 - Whoever Asked Me.	183
Poem 88 - Unbeatable.	185
Poem 89 - Undefeated.	187
Poem 90 - Crazy Love.	189
Poem 91 - Between Demons.	191
Poem 92 - The Essence of Myself.	193
Poem 93 - The Other Side.	195
Poem 94 - Reflections.	197
Poem 95 - Lost.	199
Poem 96 - Change.	201
Poem 97 - I Can Only Create.	203
Poem 98 - Selfish Love.	205
Poem 99 - The Risk of Loving You.	207
Poem 100 - Lost Souls.	209

Poem 101 - Dreaded Love. 211
Poem 102 - Who Doesn't Feel Me?..213
Poem 103 - What You Assume. 215
Book Review Request..217
Booklist...219

Title Page

Disenchanted: Poems by Rowan Knight
By Rowan Knight
Copyright © Rowan Knight, 2019 (1st Ed.) All Rights Reserved.
Published by 22 Lions Bookstore and Publishing House

About the Publisher

About the 22 Lions Bookstore:
www.22Lions.com
Facebook.com/22Lions
Twitter.com/22lionsbookshop
Instagram.com/22lionsbookshop
Pinterest.com/22lionsbookshop

Introduction

This book presents a collection of poems inspired on alchemy, love and ancient philosophies, while portraying a critical attitude towards common social values and their true meaning inside the cycles of an existence filled with turmoil.

In doing so, the author seeks to explain where chaos and balance, as well as order, find themselves. Because, according to him, it is in the combination of observations and emotions that a divine attribute is gained by the seeker of such qualities.

From this perspective onward, more is added, for there is a paradox continually being portrayed between the positive and the negative, common in each one of us, with its relations between happiness and despair, but also truth and illusion, as well as disenchantment and fantasy.

Through this approach, an awakening of emotions pointing at the different stages of consciousness is proposed, and this while stripping the reader from guilt and prejudice, but foremost, naivety.

Poem 1 - The Death of a Rose.

I found a rose
    of a bright red,
and one day,
far from expected,
the rose became dark as lead.
Upon a closer contemplation,
foretelling the death of my dear rose,
I dropped a tear in the night,
but the rose remained unmoved,
and, within my sight,
unchanged.
And yet, inside of me,
I felt scared,
and also confused,
for I could not understand
why this rose of mine
had succumb
to such ungrateful descend.
In this overwhelming darkness,
I felt alone and deprived,
for it was permeated
with an unbearable void,
which could only be filled,
whenever more tears dropped,
for what had finished,
while awakening in me something deeper

ROWAN KNIGHT

— a more profound meaning;
and my heart was beating faster,
as I was realizing
what couldn't be avoided;
I was being spiritually pressed,
towards the chaos of my soul,
filled with emotional turmoil.
Now into waterfalls
my tears had turned,
while more within me was unfold,
brought forth
by what had been suppressed.
And in front of the rose I shouted
due to the heat of what within me battled;
and down I went,
deeper into my pain;
the entirety of which
I struggled in vain.
I finally died a spiritual death,
and accepted to confront my fate,
while surrendering to this state.
And this is when my rose died,
and the petals fell on the ground,
while its roots begun to rotten,
for its purpose had been fulfilled,
never to be forgotten.
The life of this rose in me perpetuated,
and in doing so was immortalized,
for it never truly vanished.
And then I understood
why my rose was never afraid,
for it was through me that it reflected
that which within me was created
— illusions making me deluded,
and in such lie keeping me fooled,

DISENCHANTED: POEMS BY ROWAN KNIGHT

while from the truth detached
and from my true self ignored.
The peaceful death of my rose,
made my entire inside revealed,
for within this death I awakened
to the love for a life once sacrificed,
and which should always be remembered,
because the love which I ended
was the same love once envisioned;
both conditions within me emerged.

Poem 2 - Just Being.

Someone was just being,
    and in my love for this person,
I trusted the feeling,
neglected any needing,
and overlooked any giving,
assuming,
that love was what I was seeing,
or thinking
and doing.
In this naiveness,
I wasn't manifesting,
for I trusted
that love was merely a feeling.
But that person was truly loving
and took such love from me away,
for I couldn't change my being,
and this to my dismay.
And now I understand,
that someone has loved me,
while seeing nothing,
not even at the end,
which ended a future
I couldn't foresee
while in another perception immersed,
despite the emotions in me stimulated.
That one who could only be,

ROWAN KNIGHT

was, in actuality,
me.

Poem 3 - What Ends.

What ends
    awakens the spirit,
and makes you reveal your heart,
while forcing from a state to depart.
Such duality that is experienced,
deceives the eyes,
towards what never existed,
or was transformed,
but merely reflected,
and for a goal changed.
And in doing so, you went
from darkness to light,
while burning from the inside,
to reveal what you tried to hide,
just to avoid such inner fight.
For such is the cycle,
behind any miracle,
depicted in any oracle:
From nothing to nothing we go,
creating meanings
which are never our own,
so that others
may also participate
in this theatre of egos,
deceived through what is known,
and forcing everyone to cooperate,

ROWAN KNIGHT

despite any will
thought to be owned.

Poem 4 - The Monk's Dichotomy.

I woke up as a monk in a monastery
    and for the first time realized
what is to be spiritually guided,
and truly believed
it was something to be sought outside.
And so, I went out of the monastery,
to then conclude
it should be accepted from the inside.
And I was stunned
for I didn't understand
God's purpose.
Therefore,
seeking His cause,
I decided to become as a god,
by becoming more than I am:
I refused to live under the sun,
and begun
to live at night
as any owl does.
But if under the sun I had no silence,
at night, I surely had no audience.
And this was the moment I realized,
that if under the sun
and outside the monastery,
I could share what I learned,
it was only under the moon

ROWAN KNIGHT

and inside the monastery,
that I could such knowledge comprehend.
I then contemplated
the concept of my spirituality
and the need to connect this duality,
and in this contemplation
I found myself before what I desired,
at the same time
that someone knocked,
and at the door
many people I received.

Poem 5 - The Monk and the Villagers.

Inspired by God,
    a monk headed to a village,
seeking to share His glory,
and there he offered roses,
but was refused with rage,
for the villagers wanted animals
before he could read a single page.
On the second day he returned
with a basket filled with fruits,
but they still refused,
and asked
for the meat of animals.
On the third day he arrived
with a basket of vegetables,
but they continued to refuse
and asking for animals to eat.
On the fourth day, an animal he slaughtered
while asking God for forgiveness,
and offered the meat to the villagers,
who were not impressed
by his agreeableness.
They now, the purest water demanded;
and on the fifth day he took
the purest he could find,
and offered it
while asking them to share.

ROWAN KNIGHT

But they drunk everything,
and now asked for wine.
He didn't have any wine,
so took it from the monastery,
and was never allowed to return;
not until he regained
a sense of respect
and morality
for what his brothers own.
The villagers were finally happy,
and as one of them he was accepted.
And he was happy too,
and allowed himself to be accepted.
But when time came to speak of God
he realized
that he wasn't blessed,
for his mind now women desired,
his heart for wilderness craved,
and his mouth for wine shouted.
He laughed
and such pleasures enjoyed,
until a sense of spirituality was needed,
but from that void
madness he got instead.
Feeling now tormented,
impulsively
one of the swords he grabbed,
and enjoyed murder,
for he found the need to slaughter.
Amidst an horrifying
and bloody massacre
within him a flame was ignited.
And when he was covered in the red
of the blood of the ones
that he barbarically killed,

DISENCHANTED: POEMS BY ROWAN KNIGHT

in the night he had silenced
after a chaos so fantastically produced,
he found the meaning
of what he was seeking.
And then he laughed again,
like a beast owning the night,
for in that darkness
he had found the light.

Poem 6 - The Unseen Gift.

I was walking one day
    when I stood upon a gift:
a collection of flowers,
so beautiful and distinct,
strange and unique,
worthy in their combination,
and of different colors.
And so, I took them in my hands,
eager to offer them to others,
and in doing so, make more friends.
Every time I returned home,
a little girl was standing there,
as if knowing I was coming.
And she was rejoicing,
for a gift she could only be smelling.
For she was blind
despite having beautiful dark eyes
and a soul that was whispering
for compassion that I couldn't be refusing.
To her I offered my first flower,
and the same I kept doing,
day after day,
for she was always waiting,
and always in the same way.
This little child of golden hair,
soft hands and glowing skin,

ROWAN KNIGHT

remained a joy to my eyes,
and so much so,
that the flowers meant nothing
when compared to the smile I was earning.
To her all these flowers
and much more was meant,
for she had a smile
capable of making me forget
everything that in this world
I resent.

Poem 7 - Twenty-two Flowers.

I had twenty-two flowers
    on top of my bed,
and every single one
was very beautiful
in a very unique way;
They delighted me
in a variety of forms,
for their perfume filled me
with different sensations,
and the shape inspired me
to different thoughts,
keeping me motivated
throughout my days;
And although such connection was unspoken,
the trust I had in them was misled,
as if for me they had kept an omen,
that was waiting further ahead.
I eventually cut myself on those flowers,
and while suffering,
I shockingly bled;
but my trauma was deeper than those scars
and to question myself that experience had led.
I then placed them in a jar,
and watched them by afar,
I noticed the similarities
making me love them as they are,

ROWAN KNIGHT

for those similarities had meanings,
like poetry unveiling my soul's secrets.
And from within the silence emerged words,
as if they were speaking to me in whispers.
They said they weren't meant to be mine
but merely show me a path to my own soul,
and teach me that through agony I could shine.
They also told me to always remember,
that when the suffering goes deeper,
the good memories become sweeter,
and can only be replaced by a better flower,
more loving than those
which made me surrender,
to illusions that made me act
like nothing more than a pretender.
And so, by saying goodbye to the flowers,
I was saying hello to myself,
and what I truly wished to attract,
for they gave me scars,
but released me from fantasy's claws.
I saw then,
and while still bleeding,
what I should be seeking;
and in a tribute to their memory,
I cleansed myself with their agony,
while watching them burn in a fire,
unveiling within me a deeper desire,
meant to make me fulfill my passion for aesthetics,
in a spiritual immortality through what is pleasant,
when love is felt like an eternal present.
Indeed, they gave me scars
after embracing me with spells,
but also did so with my delusions,
which were now being abandoned,
with such flowers that the flames consumed.

Poem 8 - The Green Rose.

In my loneliest moment
    I found myself tormented,
after losing the last thing I had
— a single flower from my backyard.
Now immersed in this suffering,
I embraced a storm driving me mad,
and lost in this confusion
outside I went,
walking in the town frustrated,
not knowing which lesson,
or punishment,
from God to me was sent.
Then, in the midst of an emptiness
I found fullness,
in the form of white roses,
as if waiting for me they were.
And I took them in the night,
when such act
couldn't be within sight.
Years then passed,
and the roses where as found,
except one,
which turned green,
creating a situation
never before seen.
I took it out to offer to anyone nearby,

ROWAN KNIGHT

and a beautiful maiden I witnessed,
who told me that this rose was hers
and such I should not deny.
She took this rose of mine,
and later became another in my life,
by becoming my wife;
until one day,
when drunk in the night,
she allowed her heart
to be stolen away,
and because of that
my white roses perished.

Poem 09 - Odin's Heir.

For a new battle I prepare
    knowing that my dearest friends
this path won't share.
And to fight again
I must become
someone
who nobody supported,
not even with a prayer,
or with kindness,
and much less a crumb;
I leave them all behind,
as they celebrate their egotism,
in love for a life of cyclic fatalism,
and march with my soul's weapons.
I observe them on the horizon
of my heart, spirit and mind,
while heading to a war against reality,
to claim for an opportunity
that won't ever be theirs:
a fortune destined to Odin's heirs.
And I do this for the love of freedom,
to claim a new kingdom,
and its spiritual treasures.

Poem 10 - Secrets of the Dark Side.

There is something to be known inside
    that remains unknown to the outside,
something that we can't recognize
but should further analyze.
For there is something unique
inside the void of what is seen,
seducing us,
towards the unseen.
There is something profound
in a realistic pain,
that within us
fear awakens,
but also towards truth leads.
There is something forgotten
in our sounds
as well as in the vibration of love,
something that the world can't remember
but to which under passion
we must surrender.
There is something pure
in human tears,
that expresses our humanity
and its needs,
unveiling a profound honesty
filled with spiritual gifts.
There is something deep

ROWAN KNIGHT

in a broken heart,
for it expresses the frustration
of wanting,
an unfound connection,
through a sensation
that promotes devotion.
There is something noble in loneliness,
for it allows trapping the demons of sin
and seeing them insane
through self-forgiveness
— a light ignited
with God's flame.
There is something of a higher importance
in abandonment,
for it allows recalling
the attributes of self-fulfillment.

Poem 11 - Meditation Under Desire.

It is the meditation under desire,
    the painful relaxation
with a lasting memory,
that allows a chance
to gain what we admire.
And there is something important about despair,
for it breaks the soul into pieces,
crashes dreams to the ground
and into action the spirit releases.
At the end,
there are always more opportunities
behind each door of unwanted silences.

Poem 12 - The Purpose of Insanity.

There is something meaningful
    about being insane,
for it allows the joy
nobody else could provide,
proving that happiness
is not locked
or dependent.
Insanity shows a new world,
where love is revealed,
even when rejected,
by those we neglected.
And insanity,
also forces us
to assimilate
different worlds
that we once wished
to eliminate.

Poem 13 - Beyond Betrayal.

Beyond betrayal
　　or the act of being denied
and even cheated,
there is a portal.
When opened with a prayer,
it unlocks a force of unlimited power.
Through this power
the Almighty manifests,
showing that He never forgets,
and His justice purifies,
even amidst the loss of hopes.

Poem 14 - When Beauty Fades Away.

There is something superior to beauty
   revealing itself when it fades away,
for it can be kept and captured
through admiration,
showing itself
in an empathic observation.
And likewise,
through the lovers' way,
beauty can be immortal,
for it is expressed in everything
that is emotional,
moved through what commitment
can reveal.

Poem 15 - The Way of the Rose.

I bought a rose
    that soon after perished.
And so, a second I acquired,
but her life also quickly vanished.
I then continued
obtaining more roses,
all of which were beautiful,
but succumbed
to the same transitions.
And this situation persisted,
until I took a look at my emotions,
which guided me
towards the roses in others,
that started being offered
whenever my house they visited.
And in respect for such gestures,
I allowed such roses
to be as they arrived,
and the life of none disappeared.
Upon seeing this,
I realized
that what fate to me does
isn't as meaningful
as what I begun,
for I can't attract the right flowers,
with a heart weighting heavy thoughts;

ROWAN KNIGHT

and only by recognizing the heart of others,
can I be as one with the expectations
that satisfy my deepest ambitions.

Poem 16 - The Surprise of Losing You.

Life is full of surprises,
    and moments
that unsurprisingly
surprise us;
and often in the heat of a touch,
we allow every moment to surprise.
We think about the future and the past,
and don't imagine forgetting the present.
But within us stays
the memory of feelings,
the memory of sensations,
the sadness of the loss of moments,
and the sad feeling
of not seeing again
what we once imagined
to come with better winds.
Losing is always harder than forgetting,
but even more difficult is suffering,
or feeling,
the suffering of those we saw disappear,
unable to anything do or change,
or, meanwhile,
be able to alter.

Poem 17 - Knowing Without Power.

It is distressing to know
without being able
to anything do;
it is hard to know
without seeing
and in the end pay
and dearly,
for everything.
It is hard to endure
what was foreseen,
when our prediction
didn't let us see
what we did not imagine
to be feeling.
Impulses, took place
in theaters of desolation,
and all because of the ignorance
that we offered as veneration.
We did this in our hunger
for a better reasoning;
for we live evil
and suffer for a good,
while the soul
we keep emptying,
in an emotional corrupting
of everything

ROWAN KNIGHT

that to us
keeps coming.

Poem 18 - I Apologize!

The slavery of the ignorant
    is the prison of the living,
dead in spirit
and alive without merit.
So may the end come to this reality
while we save its fundamentality;
may the universe expand
and in its greatness
bring everything to an end.
For if the end of all things
is in the beginning of time,
the now of our all
is all we need for now.
And this means living love eternally
while what couldn't be changed
must be forgiven permanently.
Therefore,
I thank you for everything
and apologize for everything,
because I loved you immensely.

Poem 19 - If You Could Contemplate.

If you could contemplate
    the wisdom that through me
you could perpetuate
and live in the company of reason,
in a timeless magnificence
of reflection...
May such magnificent virtues,
to the insensitive nothing
but unreal flavors,
through the invisible deliver
what is irresistible
— a sweet taste of contemplation,
soft taste of existence,
in a continuous spiral
without desolation.
May the vision clouded
by dubious practices,
through my spirit without you,
offer the heart,
and this body give to sacrifices,
for in love I found my petrification.
Morbidus factus
in gathered realities;
In factus insanus
because of our emotions.

Poem 20 - Curse.

I loved you
    and stopped loving you,
but managed to forgive myself.
It is you who suffers now,
for a great love of the past.
I left you forever,
in your pain
— your curse,
that will eternally last.
Those devilish attributes
today consume you in thoughts.
But do suffer
to receive my love,
and show me
how insecurity trembles,
show me that consciousness
is restless;
and show me your regrets,
because in my heart I call for you,
but through your suffering
I feel no remorses.

Poem 21 - A Prisoner of Insanity.

You are sick,
    insane,
and this is what allows me to forgive
for what has been done,
as I don't want to think that you are evil,
although such is very real,
just as much as your incapacity to heal.
You're a prisoner of your own insanity;
such is the cycle of your psychopathy,
that in such a scheme arrested you,
placing you where you are today,
and justifying
why you can't love in any way.

Poem 22 - Entanglement.

I entered your mind
    and persisted;
I went as deep as I could,
and got lost;
because you are insane.
Nothing about you is consistent
but an entanglement,
of pain,
and resentment,
without anything set,
and without a light of happiness
to which you can submit,
to your own contempt.
That's why there are no grounds for loyalty
and with love you can't be happy.
But it is not my mission to save you,
although I could and can do that;
I have the power to set you free.
But we don't have love
when living in this terror.
Rather this is a scenario
of something impossible,
in which I tried to save
what from the start was an error.

Poem 23 - Ascension.

What is beautiful
  you could not see,
and maybe never will,
because beauty
is beyond suffering.
It is the gift of resisting
the windstorms of conflict,
necessary
for an understanding,
at the end of which
comes tenderness.
One day it remains,
once we find the end
of our dreams,
the desired land,
in the path towards awareness,
and of this its highest ascent,
despite our many fears.

Poem 24 - World of Sinners.

What a world this is
of crossed relationships,
of betrayals and betrayers,
and misunderstood feelings;
where everyone thinks of themselves
as fate's victims,
and not even the holiest
are rid of any guilt.
From pain to pain
I too got lost;
and from defeat to defeat
I won myself,
unknowingly being guided
in a life that nowhere leads,
when happiness is not mine.

Poem 25 - Being Someone I'm Not.

I want to rise high in my emotions
    not to fall into any temptations.
I want to rise high in my spirituality
to feel no more evil in this reality.
I want to be happy and fulfilled,
not to regret what I did.
I want to be my true self today,
not to avoid the past of yesterday,
or those I sent away,
and the relationships,
that couldn't last.
I want to be who I am not,
to be the one I forgot
in that distant past.

Poem 26 - The Desire You Chose.

I wished to die,
    but didn't want
to be killed by love;
I wished to be happy,
but didn't want
to be responsible
for such happiness;
I wished not to suffer,
but didn't want
to be the one
eliminating
this suffering;
I wished to love,
but didn't want
having to love
to be loved;
I wished,
but didn't considered
that desire
has to be desired.

Poem 27 - How to Love Someone.

Love is not something you receive,
    but something you give,
and so it builds,
in the feeling that is granted
when love is wanted.
Love is great in itself;
It does not need to be analyzed.
Give that you will receive,
and in receiving,
to give more you will want,
because you'll be feeling
more deeply.

Poem 28 - Lovely.

Loving,
    is he who sees
without seeing,
and believes
without believing,
aiming for what he does not have,
while having what never comes,
and in such way remains,
serene in himself,
quiet in the waiting without waiting,
and for less never despairing;
such is the perfect soulmate
— affectionate.

Poem 29 - The Way of the Lost.

Beauty,
      lust,
the path of cleverness,
the pride of being,
and the peace of staying
in such state of living;
such is the way of the lost
who aren't found
in the state of existence
but rather in an absence
of consciousness,
in which their unawareness
shows in itself a complete essence.
With that they rejoice
and without it they despair.

Poem 30 - The Seductive Demon.

I met a demon
    with seductive legs
and she seduced me
with her seductive way;
and I was seduced astray.
Then the demon told me
that she could not love me
and I helped her surrender;
and in this delivery,
my soul she surrendered;
and to hell with her I descended,
to prove I wasn't a fool,
that what we had was real,
and as much as what we could feel.
But I started to burn,
and the demon left me abandoned
saying it was me she loved
and it was me she truly desired,
but forever a demon she remained,
and could never be changed.

Poem 31 - The Fear of The Feared.

I saw a werewolf
    running from an armed hunter
with silver bullets;
and he was terrified,
asking to let him get away,
so that death wouldn't come his way.
I saw a vampire,
running away from an armed farmer
with garlic and stake;
and he was scared,
asking for a place to hide,
promising not to bite.
I saw a demon
fleeing from an armed priest,
with a cross and holy water;
and he panicked,
remaining hidden,
right next to me.
I saw a beautiful woman
who appeared to me
without the need to escape,
like an angel without wings;
and she loved me,
and with me stayed;
and in this way
my life she ended.

Poem 32 - Wandering.

In the landscape of my memories,
    I wander into oblivion,
to rediscover peace;
that feeling
that nothing was in vain.
I disappear here,
without seeing anything,
and without worrying;
because I just want peace
of a life of war
where the enemies
where always
inside my own heart.
I walk through me,
watching these pains
and forget who I am
and all my passions,
because I can't be
without the act of loving,
and I am nothing
without love still remaining,
because I can't be
without being.

Poem 33 - The Mask.

Forgive me,
      because I'm crazy.
No, don't forgive me.
Rather set me free,
because I'm crazy.
No, don't set me free.
Rather understand me,
because I'm crazy.
No, don't understand me.
Rather forget me,
because I'm crazy.
No, don't forget me.
Rather ignore me,
because I'm crazy.
No, don't ignore me.
Rather respect me,
because I'm crazy.
No, don't respect me.
Rather love me
because I'm crazy.
No, don't love me.
Rather desire me,
because I'm crazy.
No, don't desire me.
Rather let me be crazy.
No, don't let me be crazy.

ROWAN KNIGHT

Rather put a mask
and pretend you're not either
as crazy as I am,
and let us pretend together
that there is no madness
for as long as we can.

Poem 34 - Unfinished World.

Such is this unfinished world,
    like my insanities
which I can only call hilarious;
for between my power's ambition
and the proper stimuli of humanity,
I laugh of my inglorious condition
that the gods proposed
for who knows,
what I do not know
or will ever know,
and so do,
what I have no idea,
and never imagined.

Poem 35 - Desire.

My desire has met your desire,
    and my mind sang with this desire
and in the burning passions
of our relationship
I got lost in a world of obsessions,
where everything which existed
was for you.
I loved you as I never loved anyone;
I loved you with all the tears
that my heart for no one
ever cried.
I loved you too much
beyond the suffering,
until my sensitive heart
stopped feeling.

Poem 36 - The Meaning of Life.

What meaning does life have
    without the love of the one we want?
What purpose has a tear
without a companion?
What sense has lost love
when we need it?
What desire I can have in living
without you by my side?
What is life,
when the one I loved,
in flames of pain,
is consumed?

Poem 37 - The Colors of Love.

Life without you
    is like colors to the blind.
And how many colors does the world have
for a lost heart?
How many colors does the rainbow have,
when the eyes do not reach
beyond a thought at sight?
How many colors does a thought have,
when darkness overshadows the soul?
How many colors can I live with,
after seeing a world now gone?
How many colors can I fill my soul with,
without the presence of a calming love?

Poem 38 - I Wish.

I wish you had loved me
    without fears;
I wish you had loved me
without the need to move away;
I wish you had loved me
without games;
I wish you had loved me
without doubts;
Because if you had loved me
with an open heart,
you would have seen a man
willing to do everything
to fulfill an uncertain destiny.
So don't give up on my love,
for I didn't give up on yours.
In my silence I abandon all suffering,
but I don't give up on what we have.
I surrender to the sacrifice
in which you put me
before this torment;
but I don't give up
on the beautiful spirituality
which only we can see.

Poem 39 - So Far and So Near.

So far and so near,
    in the morning,
thinking of you,
I awake.
At night,
longingly,
I try to fall asleep.
During mid-afternoon,
tears steal my peace,
in a suffocating grip;
and in the middle of the night
my mind is stolen by despair,
in a devilish torment.
And so my soul burns for you
without ever forgetting you;
daily and without hope,
my spirit calls for you
and nothing reaches,
as I remember our moments,
as I remember our dreams
and get lost in endless pains,
suppressing me without mercy.
Despite the many women I meet,
how can I fall in love again?
After with you having seen
a world beyond hope,

ROWAN KNIGHT

how can I now refuse you
and desire again?

Poem 40 - If You Loved Me.

If you loved me like I love you
    you wouldn't fear my love.
If you loved me like I love you
with me you would do the impossible,
and this pain eliminate.
I'm not the evil you see
and not even the weaknesses you encounter.
I am the dream in which you believe;
I am the angel who lifts you up to the highs;
I am all that you wanted for your world.
I am this reality and much more
filling that anxious heart of yours.
I am the salvation of your lost soul
and I am a gentle lover.
If you know that I love you,
what else do you expect then?
If in my dreams I call for you,
why wait in your loneliness?

Poem 41 - I Don't Believe You.

I loved you
    for as long as I could,
I loved you
and giving up I never would,
I loved you
and I still do love you,
but I call for you no more.
When on cold nights
my heart for you longs,
I scream louder
with memories
and say to myself:
I must not feed hopes.
I don't believe you.
How can I believe,
if in you a great dream I saw,
but everything you did
was make me discredit my own?

Poem 42 - Your Sword.

You took my heart,
    and raised it to the highs,
and from a cliff of pains
you released it into thorns.
You've abused my sufferings
and in that joy
your heart felt calm,
because, in fact,
you belong to an icy tower,
where you keep your cold heart
and allow no one to take it.
The sword,
with which you pierced my heart,
the same sword you twisted after jabbing,
today is the sword I use to annihilate you,
insensitive demon that arrived in my life to hurt,
that cried for my love and pity
but doesn't deserve any clemency.

Poem 43 - Bewitched.

Bewitched by your perfume,
    I became yours beyond infinity.
My soul surrendered
to your floral gaze
and forever
in your spirit I died.
That's why I hate you;
because I am your prisoner.
That's why I feel anger,
and frustration;
because forever
I am in your hand.
You own my destiny,
because I love you
more than I love the divine.
You own me
and because of you
I am like this,
a dying lover
eagerly waiting
that love of yours;
or that you quickly
annihilate me.

Poem 44 - Queen of the Dark.

Rejoice in your throne,
    oh Queen of the dark,
because your life includes nothing
but the forgotten ones.
I will not be your lover,
because I belong to another kingdom,
but maybe your slave;
because from my conscience
I am oblivious.
We are enemies,
but I've surrendered,
because I'm from a better world
and got lost from it.
We are enemies,
because the love
that I always felt for you
feeds my eternal pain.

Poem 45 - Affliction.

You leave me
    until I leave you
and then you say
that I own your heart.
But why you recognize it
only in distress
and before that
you systematically say no?
I'm letting our love die
without the water and the sun
that saw it rise.
But I gave a lot of myself
and you did nothing to help;
so, today, I leave our love like this,
slowly dying,
like a withering flower,
in the fading thoughts,
in a pain without comparison,
of my deepest affliction;
I'm afraid of losing you,
but I don't know
what else to do.
In many moments I suffered
and few I remember
when I laughed.
And smiles...

ROWAN KNIGHT

were you sincere?
I believe those moments
where for you without meanings
because you cannot love.
You can only gaslight with desires.

Poem 46 - Who Can Free Me?

It is you my love;
    It is you who can set me free.
For in what we have I am your prisoner;
I am yours in every sight of mine,
I am yours and always in the morning,
and I am yours when falling asleep.
So I faint in this ardor,
a longing fire,
that makes me shudder
with every breath of aspiration,
while I wish you in vain
and your lips I want to feel,
to calm my heart
from this pain.

Poem 47 - Slayer.

I showed you love,
    but you refused;
in darkness you recognized yourself better,
because light means for you pain;
and the demonic power you preferred
to manipulate me without limits.
But love can't be arrested
and that's why I left unharmed;
not without ceasing to love you first,
because only to you I wished to surrender,
and that, despite seeing you
as my slayer.

Poem 48 - Complicity.

It's a complicity
  this silence of ours,
in which we want
but deny our voice,
while resigning
to our pride;
or is it fear of a relationship
that is addictive,
— abstract frame
of diffuse feelings,
which should have ended
but chase us,
although without any uses?
I wake up thinking of you
and it's been like this
since I saw you.
But you are poison to me,
even though I appreciate the feeling
that heals the heart from your pains,
whenever you hurt me with regrets
and in doing so
show me your evilness.

Poem 49 - Empty Promises.

You promised,
 insisted,
repeated
and lied.
You've created hopes,
emotions,
and betrayals.
You have wrapped me
in poisons,
of intrigues
and torments,
through frustrations
in which I lost direction
to the cause of how it all began,
and evaporated between smokes
of illusions that today I want to forget
because I no longer want to see you.
The deep pain I feel,
for recognizing myself
in a world that won't recognize me,
makes me hate the function
of all that love could be,
because everything is given
to be forgotten
in a cycle in which everything is wished
but lost.

ROWAN KNIGHT

It is a war for compassion
without any empathy
or acknowledgment of reason,
in the unrecognized unreality
of this illusion
believed to be true.

Poem 50 - The Victory of the Vanquished.

The memory of promises
    of empty hearts,
are like endless melodies
holding feelings
eager for more,
aspiring to future moments,
while enjoying perfumes
of whom in memory stayed
and in the heart was kept.
Through this reality of mine,
something calls for you,
because my heart
despairs for peace.
Given the robbery that I lived
and from which nothing comes back,
I know I can just give more,
so that I might not give too much.
I long for the future
as longing in the present,
remembering the past,
sadly remembered
and lost
to an unexpected future;
stuck between my memory
and the desire,
I die for the present

ROWAN KNIGHT

and who I am,
to be who I never will,
because in spirit I want to end
everything that began
but no one ended.
So I give you more
to recover and win
furthermore.

Poem 51 - Adrift.

I feel as an empty boat,
    aimlessly,
lost, ...
a boat without a sailor,
seeking for a meaning
to an undecided purpose,
in the absence of reasoning
which I envision
being lost.
I seek direction
in this retreat
in which I find myself rendered,
thinking of you
and only to you surrendered.
A corrupt purchase this is,
which charged me more than winds
in storms over ships,
of angry gods
acting on unprotected sailors
sold to themselves.
Ships and sailors
never needed direction,
but compassion
from the tides
and who controls them
and on them devours.

ROWAN KNIGHT

A bad sailor I am
for trusting demons
that in my sea of emotions
came and sacrificed everything
least the soul that remained.

Poem 52 - Where I Found Myself.

I found in love
    the invisible response
of a repeated pain;
I found in peace
the illusory lie
of a transient truth;
I found in us
the lie of my words
— fruits of voiceless thoughts.
I found in the pain the truth
about a soul's sacrifices,
resulting from a fervent love;
I found in mismatch
the lack of reason in love
— result of who knows no other;
I found in you
whom I never wanted for me
— a truth that before I'd never seen.

Poem 53 - The Muse.

I know that you exist
    and I wait for you as if for me,
because without you I'm not
what I want to be
and do not know
how to exist.
I dream with a reality
that for now is not,
aspiring for a being
that I cannot yet see.
I see myself
as I see you
and identify myself
as I identify you;
being who I am
so that you may be
whom I desire
— muse of my world;
I fear as much as I want you,
while boasting myself
for having you in a dream
in which within
it improves itself,
to lead me
to a greater perfection
where my mind flies

ROWAN KNIGHT

and I vanish for you.
I surrender to the dream
of knowing you exist
and wait for the time to see;
because the alternative
is made of many waits
where in neither
I ever felt expected.
You're a muse of happiness
that feeds my creativity.

Poem 54 - Unable to Be.

In my heart lies a pain,
    which bottom I can't see,
don't want to see
or even feel,
and much less know.
But, at the root of my being
lies the solution;
the solution to this pain
that I cannot see.
Grew like a weed
and within me
consumes me
and now I'm afraid
to see it
or even feel it.
I know that one day
it will completely consume me
because I stopped feeling it.
From pain to pain,
I built my suffering,
and have built my cross.
This cross has nails
of those who have crucified me;
but some are larger than others,
because some hurt me more.

Poem 55 - The Cross of Light.

Cross of light,
    light of my darkness,
and from darkness cross,
in which I'll disappear.
As who could not be,
I will be so
— an end
of what was nothing,
overshadowed,
by what I wanted to become.
I cannot love,
because in this prison I can't be.
I cannot love you,
because I can't live in this way.
As such, is this demonic world,
cruel and illusory,
in which I was born to perish,
and which condemns me now
to a life that made me grow
for just, as an animal,
sacrifice me
and destroy.
It's a cruel world
and inhuman,
full of insignificant creatures,
but would I be inhumane

ROWAN KNIGHT

for considering you the same?
I believe that this inhumanity
is just a reflection of the inability
to love you in this virtual world.

Poem 56 - Reverberations.

My life
    is equalized
by reverberations
and composed of thoughts,
merged
on themselves,
as sounds
that harmonious strings
in a guitar can be heard.
This is the image
continuously alternating
of my existence
— illusory reality;
I don't love you,
and I can't love you,
because of your world
I am not,
nor ever have been,
and nor could I ever be.
I'm just a stranger
between ghosts of the past
and desires of the living;
lost,
as aimlessly souls;
a bridge between worlds
whose waters comprise

ROWAN KNIGHT

all my reincarnations;
many more than any being
in this world
and parallel ones
could know.

Poem 57 - Hidden World.

Come to me hidden world,
    as today I'm your ruler,
and show me
what I can now see!
Come to me grief
because you're from my soul
and only I can love you!
Teach me again
about the path that is beyond,
and to hate everything I here see,
with all my heart!
Feed the hate I feel for these humans
worse than their animals,
because they reject honesty,
kill without mercy,
and venerate violence.
Teach me to see their wishes
and listen to their thoughts,
to know more reasons
to reject them!
Teach me the truth
that only my brothers see,
so that I may never love any human
and forever despise them.

Poem 58 - The Love I Fear.

Two types of love I know
    but only one I recognize.
Never will I know human love
because I don't understand,
or comprehend,
this love of such nonsense.
May mine
protect me from the other,
as in this trap I'm weak
and vulnerable
to a cursed world.
May compassion
depart from me,
because in this virus
my thoughts fade,
and I'm vulnerable
to an immense
endless cruelty...

Poem 59 - Treacherous.

Treacherous creatures
   that I came to know
so that my own kind
may be able to identify,...
May death come on these weak
disguised with arrogant attitudes
and glorious stories
about winners and losers,
of those immortalized in leadership
and the ones in sacrifice forgotten.
May the dishonesty
of those that in lies hide,
be the plague of their bodies
and worms in them grow,
proportionally to their cruelty
and adverse actions
against humanity!

Poem 60 - The Fate of the Damned.

Despicable is this damn race
 of a false god,
selfish and arrogant,
and of his illusory light
which overshadowed the best
among Men.
A God of gods,
of angels and saints,
can only be a liar
as any human is,
when imposing to his brothers,
and denying them independence
of mind and reason,
or even thoughts,...
ignorance
of whom calls this faith.

Poem 61 - I Hate this Existence.

I hate this body of mine
    and my existence,
because I hate this planet
to where I was sent.
But I grieve, however;
and suffer deeply,
because I cannot love here.
In a world without love
without true love, as I know it,
it is impossible to feel in truth.
Yet, tears escape me
through a throbbing heart,
sensitive and weak,
whenever I remember the love
I left behind,
when about it I think;
because it was more real
than what I feel here today.
In another reality
where I've known it,
I've lived and shared it.
For there is a world
of a brotherhood,
with harmony, truth
and compassion,
and much more than this,

ROWAN KNIGHT

as it's another reality,
incomparable,
to what this allows
within the limits
of the imagination.
But I came here
and from here cannot leave
until my mission ends,
and this physical shell
of slow arms and legs,
in a paralyzed world,
by ignorance and violence,
I leave behind.
In that moment only
can I love again;
and so,
I hope for that day,
and long for that period,
that only this life of suffering
could make me remember.

Poem 62 - Because I Cannot Love.

Here,
         in this world,
I cannot love.
There is no love,
when everything is material;
when hatred and injustice,
envy and fear,
prevent the truth
of being,
blooming
and prospering.
This is not my world.
Thus, you can try to love me,
but you can never grow
as me when loving you;
for I love you more
than what you could understand
with the love you know.
You'll never have my love,
as you wish;
not in this reality,
because I cannot love you
as you love me.

Poem 63 - I Believe You are Good.

I believe you are good.
   You've just been bitten
by too many vampires
and they've ruined
your nice mood;
they have erased the beauty in your eyes.
And I wish I could be dark and untrue,
so I could still be with you.
But I am not,
and that's why I'll have to leave,
in order not to be forgot;
I leave in order for you to achieve
the freedom of the darkness
in which you've lost your kindness.
I know you can be saved
because I've seen this kind light
behind emotions
that so much had me amazed;
I've seen it when inside you there's a fight.
You want to love,
but you can't love.
You want to have love,
but you can't have love.
Darling wife of spiritual paths,
exorcise your pain through wraths!
Think of me and miss me!

ROWAN KNIGHT

Don't stop loving
and you'll rise above;
and on the top of that dark hill,
you'll see me near the sun.
There, you'll have my heart again
if you so believe.
Because, apart from the light
from which you run,
my heart is always yours
and for you I'll always retrieve.

Poem 64 - Please Be Free!

Please be free,
    so that in sharing love we may be.
I love you.
Please don't forget!
Use this knowledge
so that your freedom may be set!
Take the pain of today,
so that you may love tomorrow!
Think of me,
but not forever,
because I don't want to be your sorrow,
whenever about us you remember.
I want to be your greatest lover.

Poem 65 - Shoot an Arrow!

Crave your teeth in my neck!
　　Do it, until my bones crack!
Can you see my smile?
Shoot an arrow at my chest!
Do it, until I feel a dying need to rest!
Can you notice my peaceful profile?
Crave on me the biggest sword you can find!
Then twist it, until this pain doesn't mind!
Can you see my loving eyes?
No, no, no...
don't give up on the rage!
Because love is powerful
and in this pain
you strengthen our cage,
and our connection never dies.
Keep giving me pain
and getting weak,
so that I can catch you forever
after you're dull
and in doing so
make you lose
with your own trick.
You are mine,
because I'm undefeated;
I'm in love
and this is something

ROWAN KNIGHT

beyond anything limited.
Love cannot die,
and you cannot kill me.
I'm in love,
and now you cannot flee.
You're mine, my love,
trapped in my emotional cage.
You're mine, my dove.
This agony is our final stage;
your rage, my joy;
your pain, my funny hobby.
Come, and surrender,
because you're mine forever.

Poem 66 - Nowadays.

Nowadays, I see...
    that my future moves with hope
when with love I can cope.
Nowadays, my spirit is free...
due to the emotional bridges we've built
between two worlds,
and without guilt.
Nowadays...
I see the strength
of every single one of these days,
and I recognize that, like you,
in life I've built my strength,
not knowing that in the process
I've also created my weakness.
I've found the perfection of life...
knowing that with you
my strength can become
my normal behavior's candlelight,
and my weakness
a way to truly create happiness.
Nowadays...
I see paths
in the joy we've set free as rays.
I see cosmic empowerment
in the embracing of two souls
building what for us shows

ROWAN KNIGHT

— an accomplishment.

Poem 67 - Our Empire.

Le monde n'est pas grand
    if in you I see a huge land.
La perfection n'est pas tout
quando vejo um eu e um tu.
Son los efectos
de las emociones,
prueba de la perfección
en las reacciones,
et aussi l'amour,
our beautiful detour,
en sentimientos
que solidifican nuestro imperio
numa beleza de eterno mistério.

Poem 68 - Come and See!

What are you doing?
    Appreciating your tears?
What are you seeing?
The pain you've created from fears?
Love is about happiness;
I have it waiting for you to accept.
But if you don't,
I'll be restless,
as I have what you reject
and you also have what I want
waiting for what I grant;
It is here!
So come!
I command you to come!
Come to me;
Come and see;
Come and love me!

Poem 69 - Omnia In Divina.

Omnia in omnibus
    sed omnia divinitus.
Omnia aequalia
et omnia in divina.
The divine
is what commands me,
for it makes everything shine,
including the love I can't see,
but is mine.

Poem 70 - Life Has Pain.

Life has pain
    but I believe nothing is in vain,
for I hope to increase love around me,
so that a purpose I may see.
I believe our path is made of love.
Otherwise, what are we here for?
To die without a door?
That isn't living;
for life is about seeing
and following the unseen,
forsaking the nonbeing
and releasing
what has not yet been.
Life is about going,
letting go
and showing
what isn't so.
Because we're here
not to plan ahead,
but to move beyond,
letting go the thread
of facing what is found.
So go and let go!
Set yourself free!
And then I'll show
what you can be.

ROWAN KNIGHT

Nothing in this world is empty,
and you're inside a higher plan
to move in a mission
and see what you must see.
There is nothing you cannot be
and this is your realization,
and so, you must ban
what isn't of a higher plan;
Let it go!
Because everything I'll show.
You cannot see,
for it isn't yet meant to be.
It's not how it works;
It works like it's supposed
in the order that in itself shows.
Let it go! Let it go!
I'll show what you need to know.

Poem 71 - What a Lie Can't Conquer.

No lie can conquer my heart
    for I'm not supposed to be torn apart.
Responsibility is sweet when accepted
but bitter when demanded.

Poem 72 - Magic.

There is magic in reality
    but can only be seen
by an eye unseen;
the one we call heart;
for it speaks sincerely
in all art.

Poem 73 - No Future Holds the Mind.

No future holds the mind
    that is alone in its pride,
because the mind is sacred,
knowing what to find
and stoping only to guide
every time that it's named,
and called
like the heart's instrument
that men must lend,
so that higher powers may
guide through the day.

Poem 74 - Saints and Sinners.

What a world this is
    of crossed loves,
of betrayers and betrayals,
of misunderstood love,
where everyone thinks they're victims,
but not even the holiest among these
are rid of their own guilt and sins.
From pain to pain I got lost
and from defeat to defeat
I owned myself,
not knowing that I walked
in a life that leads to nothing
when happiness is not mine.

Poem 75 - Incomprehensible.

Lost in emotions
    I find myself defeated.
Love has defeated me
like never before I've been defeated;
and in this pain I wished to die
for the pleasure of loving,
because I want nothing more
than to love and be loved,
and feel the powerful force of passion;
a strength that brings us down completely
and make us feel spiritual,
immortal,
like the sea,
that without form
and without pretense
is complete
in its immensity
and remains eternal
in its instability,
that in no way
removes its identity.
Such is love,
that drives all emotions,
make us climb high
and destroys us
with an inhuman calm,

ROWAN KNIGHT

a misunderstood state of mind
— incomprehensible peace!

Poema 76 - The Nothing You Represent.

Lies
   that are confused in truths;
Feelings
that get confused in insanities.
So you are,
strange creature that I loved
believing to be real.
But you are not!
You are but an animal,
a strange being
in a struggle for survival,
unable to love,
unable to be normal;
or maybe not,
if nothing exists within you,
but what you never were,
even if you mention it.
You do not feel love.
You do not love me.
You are what you are
— a nothing,
in search of everything,
all that you are not,
because you can't be anything.

Poem 77 - Why Love?

Love is big in itself.
    It does not need to be analyzed.
Give that you will receive
and by receiving
to give more you will want;
for you will feel more too.
So we are,
not just animals
but rather spiritual beings
of loving ambitions
and spirited needs.

Poem 78 - A Thousand Sensations.

Oh, beautiful woman
    who steals my emotions
and enchants me
in a thousand sensations.
You stole my thoughts
and prevented me from writing novels,
but you can't stop me from writing poetry,
because in poems my emotions fly
and in them I conquer you,
For I express a joy in these,
an emotion that doesn't get stuck,
and in releasing this sensation
I come to you,
in an energy you don't see,
an energy that is already here.

Poem 79 - An Intrigue.

You know,
    you feel
and you can know
what is there
to be perceived;
but you get confused
because you do not see in me
what you expect to see;
You can only feel a projection
of a strong emotion,
an energy that feeds your body
and lifts your heart,
and therefore intrigues you;
and in the intrigue you remain,
without being able to see
what the heart feels,
such a strong emotion
that from me emerges
and in you follows,
to complete a cycle,
a magic dynamic
only ours,
that the eyes do not see,
but a heart can feel,
and intrigues us,
more you than me;

ROWAN KNIGHT

and I see
your instability,
even if my eyes
you deceive;
because I own my world
and it's a hidden world
that you don't understand
but comes to you
in a way
you do not comprehend.
In this world I'm king
and you my sovereign,
because I control
the energy of this world
where you can only feel
and realize,
without there entering;
and in that sensation
you are intrigued
without knowledge.
And yet,
you also trap me,
because of your beauty.

Poem 80 - Pride.

My pride
    met your pride
and proud we lived
in a proud love,
until you lost your pride
and exchanged me for others
to keep your image;
and then became recreated,
on a new journey
to keep your pride,
for only that is pleasant to you.
We didn't know
how to maintain ourselves
but at least you kept your pride.

Poem 81 - Lucifer.

I spoke with Lucifer
    and he asked me to deliver
a message to God;
and in return I asked:
Why me?
To which he answered:
Because you could not observe
what I will give you,
not even if it was already yours.

Poem 82 - Stupidity.

I am studying stupidity
    with an intelligence
allowed by ignorance;
and I see
what those who hurt me
also saw.
I understand their evilness,
but I do not understand
my numbness,
that stupidity
did not make possible
to detect.
I just see
what was left;
and I feel stupid
for before not seeing
and not realizing
how stupid I was
and how stupid
I keep being.

Poem 83 - Seeing Myself in You.

I wonder
    if I am who I am,
or an appearance
of what was left
— unmelted tears
that my heart hailed
and pains suffered
that my soul crystallized.
So I am,
trapped in an icy castle
from the pain once passed,
until with love
everything is melted
and again myself I can see
in the eyes of another,
cloistered in what is left of me.

Poem 84 - Dispensable.

In the imbecilities of life
    I found a reason to live;
in expendable people,
a reason to leave;
and in these words,
a way to avoid
sins,
which otherwise,
I could not stop.

Poem 85 - The Damnable.

I don't know if you're stupid,
    evil or tasteless;
You are certainly empty
of feelings
and emotions;
You clearly don't love me,
because you don't know the meaning
of losing the opportunity to love,
and learning
to respect another person.
Therefore,
you will never receive,
no true love,
nor real affection;
but instead live the illusion
of broken relationships
before you start them;
damnable
since the beginning;
You will be used
as you use others
and you will die
old and lonely,
as nothing
but dust.

Poem 86 - Illusory Love.

You knew how to conquer me
 and how to love me,
but you abandoned
between lies
and memories
that today are no more
than stories
with which I build the truth;
and in this way
get lost in your insanity.
In the mirage
of an illusory love
I drank the toxic waters
of your passion
and then got stuck
in disappointment
of a relationship that ends today,
by ending with me mercilessly.
You have my heart
captive,
without forgiveness.
However,
I can only be blamed
for loving you
and just for that
I deserve to be condemned,

ROWAN KNIGHT

for no one should love
whom does not love in return.

Poem 87 - Whoever Asked Me.

The one who asked me not to deceive,
    deceived.
The one who asked me not to lie,
lied.
The one who asked me not to assault,
assaulted.
The one who asked me not to cheat,
cheated.
And today, I suffer for allowing
what to me was never allowed.

Poem 88 - Unbeatable.

You left me with anguish
 to leave towards a winning pose
and land
on the penis of another man,
and then spread your vulture's wings,
upon landing
on your indecency;
devilish spirit,
longing for my decay.
You won't take me away
to the world of the dead,
because even though
you did tear my heart out
with your thirst for passion
and hunger for my flesh,
I laugh at my situation
and free myself to insanity
without fearing
freeing myself,
to your evil,
because with it I laugh.

Poem 89 - Undefeated.

I will never accept defeat;
    for I'm not defeated
when laughing.
And this I do today;
I laugh non-stopping;
I laugh at my humiliation,
I laugh at my loneliness,
I laugh at all the losses
that you made me lose,
just to tell you:
you did not win
and you'll never win,
because I laugh at everything:
me, you,
of what was
and what will not be.
I laugh at my end;
Therefore you can't win,
for never shall my spirit
you destroy.
I'm invincible;
and the more pain I feel,
the more I laugh,
because this is my instinct
— I am the undefeated.

Poem 90 - Crazy Love.

I lived a love
     of mad passions
and loved madly.
This love was also a war
and I warred ardently.
From all this madness
I wanted to break free
and today, with nostalgia,
I try to remember it
because I still want it;
but no more than happiness,
which I start to find again
and comes from within,
in all my self-esteem
unlike any other;
because only mine I truly was,
only to myself I can be delivered,
with a spirit I can't transgress,
but only love in its fullness.

Poem 91 - Between Demons.

Between the devil
    who in love violated
and the one
who in friendship misled,
I hide from what sought me,
without forgetting
what remained in me
— remnants of a hell
that has ended,
but stole part of me from me,
to turn me into someone
I don't know,
after fooling me
with whom I've known.

Poem 92 - The Essence of Myself.

In the hands of the devil
    God delivered me,
knowing I would never be defeated,
and thus He trained me
so that in pain I would know
that nothing about me has ended.
I am who I am
— everything and nothing,
that is protected in his God,
no matter what burned inside;
for I never lose the essence
of all that I am and is mine.
Due to all of this,
I am superior to the hell
that goes through me
and can never take from me
the smallest portion of my soul.

Poem 93 - The Other Side.

You broke my spirit
    with the greatest falsehood,
the best mask ever created;
it is the mask of love,
the one you betrayed me with
to leave me in this pain,
completely alone;
But I feed and rejoice
on the happiness of my madness,
and I'm proud
to have created it
with the ingredients
of your insanity
which sustained me
and fed deep dreams
that broke my spirit,
to allow me to visualize
a new universe;
And so I thank you,
for sharing such insanity,
and allowing me,
to unravel the other side
of my own sanity.

Poem 94 - Reflections.

Dear love of mine,
 reflection of what I am not,
of what I never was
and always hated,
in you I learned to see
what I never believed:
That I am more
than what I ever thought I could be.
In such insanity I find myself
with the darker side of me
and rediscover the purpose
to which I came into this world.
So I thank you for that,
all the suffering,
and also the hating;
because in your hate
I learned to be more sober
through the unusual state
of my madness without parity,
and with which I recognize today
my own duality.

Poem 95 - Lost.

I lost in fantasy,
    my hope;
I lost in confidence,
my power;
I lost in a girl,
my creativity;
I lost in vanity,
my commitment;
I lost in excellent performance,
my patience;
I lost in excellence
what I have.
And what do I have now?
I have you,
to forget
what I don't wanna see
and philosophize
about what I can't
and I shouldn't be able to do.

Poem 96 - Change.

We think it is simpler to change
 and thus our reality transform;
we believe that, if we transform,
the social reality surrounding us changes.
Such is the illusion,
because the language of the heart
is universal;
Nothing changes
without a changing in the change,
a change that involves
the one who changes
in the change
in which he dissolves.

Poem 97 - I Can Only Create.

I can't control how I feel
and will always be cornered
by feelings,
which guide me
to unpredictable moments,
where I love,
hate, destroy
and even cry,
for whom I loved
and had to destroy,
because I couldn't love,
because I wasn't loved
and only alone
I could stay.
I'm a nullification of truths
resulting from my ramblings,
inconsolable inspirations
that pull me to the message
that I must transmit;
I'm a worker of the divine
and that I cannot deny;
for my soul depends on it
in an intended contract
that is as eternal as destiny.
I was born to create
and not to love,

ROWAN KNIGHT

but I love what I create
and I can love
whoever loves me,
because love can also manifest,
in what in me is manifested.

Poem 98 - Selfish Love.

Who loves me
    for selfish reasons
from my heart pieces steals
like a thief in the middle of the night,
without being discovered,
until the loss is so much
that all that remains
is an empty heart;
emptied of my lost self,
emptied of fading dreams,
emptied of my own feelings,
which meanwhile become dark
like the clouds of a storm
that predict the depression
with which I will have to live.

Poem 99 - The Risk of Loving You.

The pain of loving
    and losing
I did not want.
With the risk of losing
I don't want to stay.
But I find myself
permanently
in this duality,
of loving
and suffering,
for refusing to lose,
for refusing to surrender
to a world of loneliness,
where I lose as well
the ability to be
— my own destiny.

Poem 100 - Lost Souls.

Lost souls unite
    on the path of evil
treading the way
for the purest,
to divert them
from their kindness;
and in this way
they can,
as you can,
make me hate
and despise you;
and it is sad,
as the sad duality we live in,
but it is also the destiny
to which you and I were born.
In a common plane
we then define our roles:
me, loving,
and you, destroying;
even though we could
learn to love as we are.

Poem 101 - Dreaded Love.

From the love I feel
    to the words I speak,
I receive the hate
of those who fear
to love me;
I receive their pain
as if in me
they could purify;
and I can't choose
any other way
but to abandon them.
I wish I could get peace
without words,
or logic,
or even reason.
I wish I could get
that calm
just with a touch of a hand,
a look,
or a smile.
I wish it was that simple,
and easy,
to destroy the energy of hate
that a broken heart feeds
and thus feed such a heart.
But if I do

ROWAN KNIGHT

I will be loved,
and I fear being loved
for those who have not
yet loved me.
I fear that reason
and for fear of reason
contrary to confusion,
I confuse those who love me.
In the anger of being lost
from something they know,
to enter the unknown,
they fear me,
attack me,
and I allow such aggression.
All I can do is have them in my hand
as I open my heart,
into which they will never enter.

Poem 102 - Who Doesn't Feel Me?

I feel confused
    for feeling
who doesn't feel me
and to me lies;
I feel lost
for liking
who doesn't like me,
but such truth denies;
I feel without truth,
because I think I fool myself
in my illusions,
without comparison or proof;
I don't understand why I'm like this,
or why I love in such a way,
or why such people come to me;
to show what I don't want
or make me see what I want?
To help develop who I am
or make me learn
about who I don't want to become?
Maybe it all comes from me
and what suits me best;
for I love
who doesn't want to love me
and I wish these
who do not want me;

ROWAN KNIGHT

maybe to stay
between thoughts that fill me,
of memories of those
than in my heart
have chosen not to remain.

Poem 103 - What You Assume.

Whenever you think I am being judged
    I am judging you;
Whenever you think you are hiding,
I am watching you;
Whenever you think you are lying,
I am analyzing you;
Whenever you think you are abandoning,
I am leaving you;
Whenever you think you are punishing,
I am deceiving you;
And once you realize these illusions,
which are fruit of your own self-deceptions,
you'll know I was never truly anywhere,
for I was never whom you thought I was,
but only an illusion of your own desires.

Book Review Request.

Dear Reader, Thank you for purchasing this book! I would love to know your opinion. Writing a book review helps in understanding readers and also has an impact on other reader's purchasing decisions. Your opinion matters. Please write a book review! Your kindness is greatly appreciated!

Booklist.

Books written by the author:
Agne: Inside the Mind of a Narcissist;
Destiny: When Your Soulmate Finds You;
Disenchanted: Poems by Rowan Knight;
Illusion: When a Nymphomaniac Falls in Love;
One Chance: 20 Short Stories with a Plot Twist and Moral Lesson;
Prophecy: A Message to Humanity;
Slave: Fulfilling a Prophecy;
Soulless: Letters to a Narcissist.

About the Publisher

This book was published by 22Lions.com.
Follow us at Facebook.com/22lions

www.ingramcontent.com/pod-product-compliance
Lightning Source LLC
Chambersburg PA
CBHW020420010526
44118CB00010B/345